I0825486

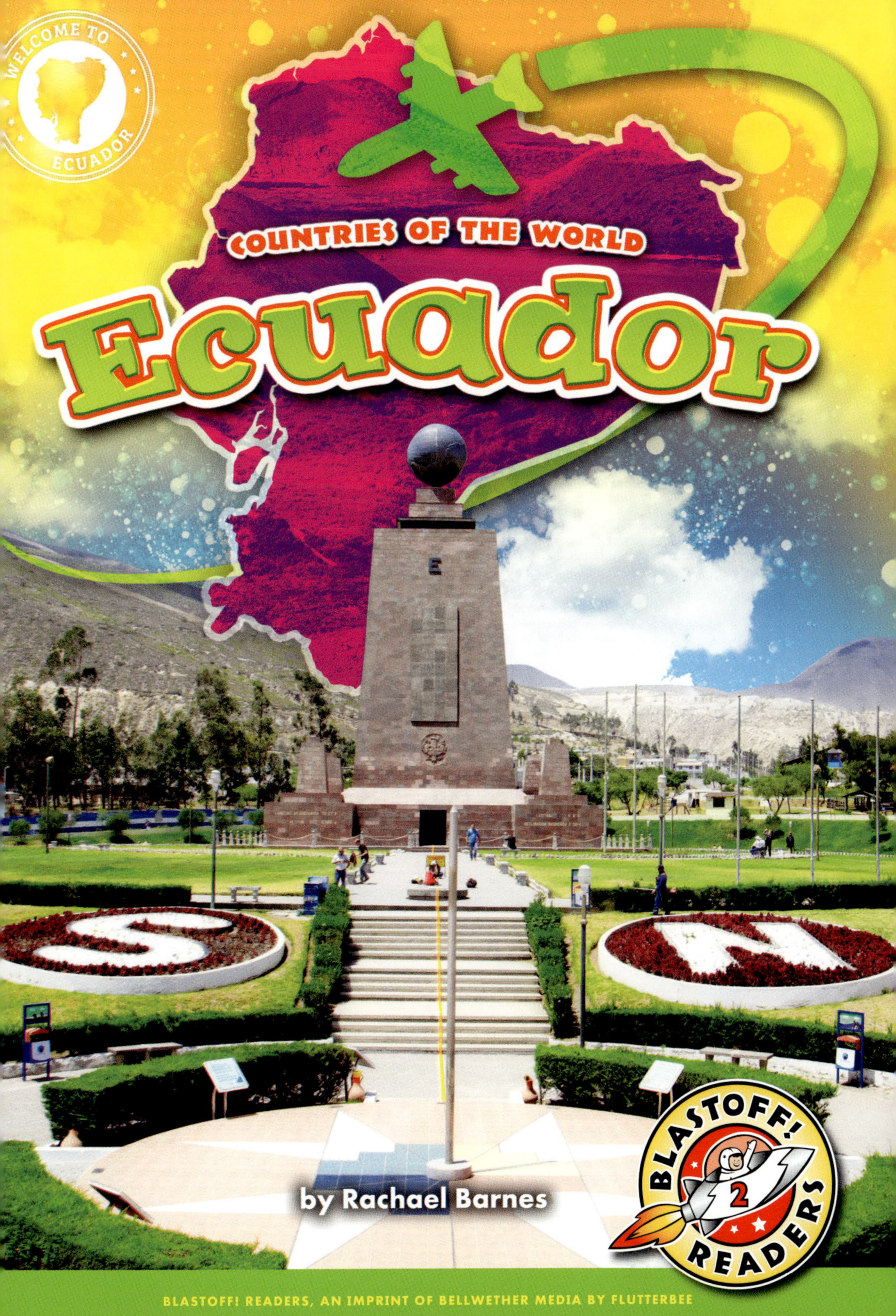

WELCOME TO
ECUADOR
COUNTRIES OF THE WORLD
Ecuador
E
by Rachael Barnes
BLASTOFF!
2
READERS
BLASTOFF! READERS, AN IMPRINT OF BELLWETHER MEDIA BY FLUTTERBEE

Blastoff! Readers are carefully developed by literacy experts to build reading stamina and move students toward fluency by combining standards-based content with developmentally appropriate text.

Level 1 provides the most support through repetition of high-frequency words, light text, predictable sentence patterns, and strong visual support.

Level 2 offers early readers a bit more challenge through varied sentences, increased text load, and text-supportive special features.

Level 3 advances early-fluent readers toward fluency through increased text load, less reliance on photos, advancing concepts, longer sentences, and more complex special features.

★ **Blastoff! Universe**

Reading Level

Grade K

Grades 1–3

Grade 4

This edition first published in 2026 by Bellwether Media, Inc.

For information regarding permission, write to Bellwether Media, Inc., Attention: Permissions Department, 3500 American Blvd W, Suite 150, Bloomington, MN 55431.

Library of Congress Cataloging-in-Publication Data is available at www.loc.gov or upon request from the publisher.

ISBN: 9798893047813 (hardcover)
ISBN: 9798893048810 (ebook)

Editor: Ashley Kuehl Designer: Brittany McIntosh

Printed in the United States of America, North Mankato, MN.

Table of Contents

All About Ecuador

Quito

Ecuador is a small country in South America. It lies on the **equator**! Quito is the capital.

Ecuador is home to over one million types of plants and animals.

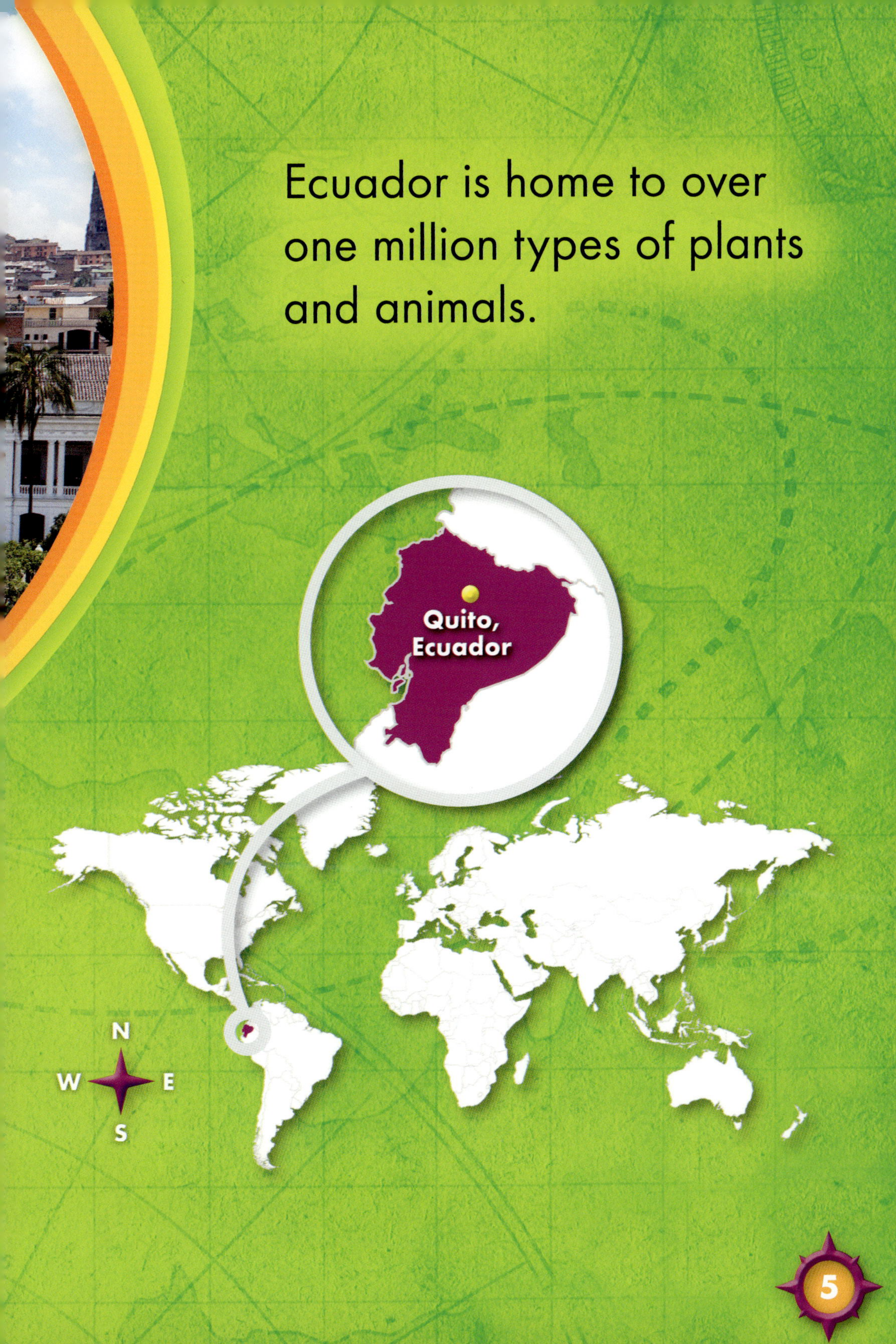

Land and Animals

Ecuador's west coast touches the Pacific Ocean. The Amazon **Rainforest** covers the east.

The Andes Mountains run through the middle of Ecuador. Some peaks are active **volcanoes**!

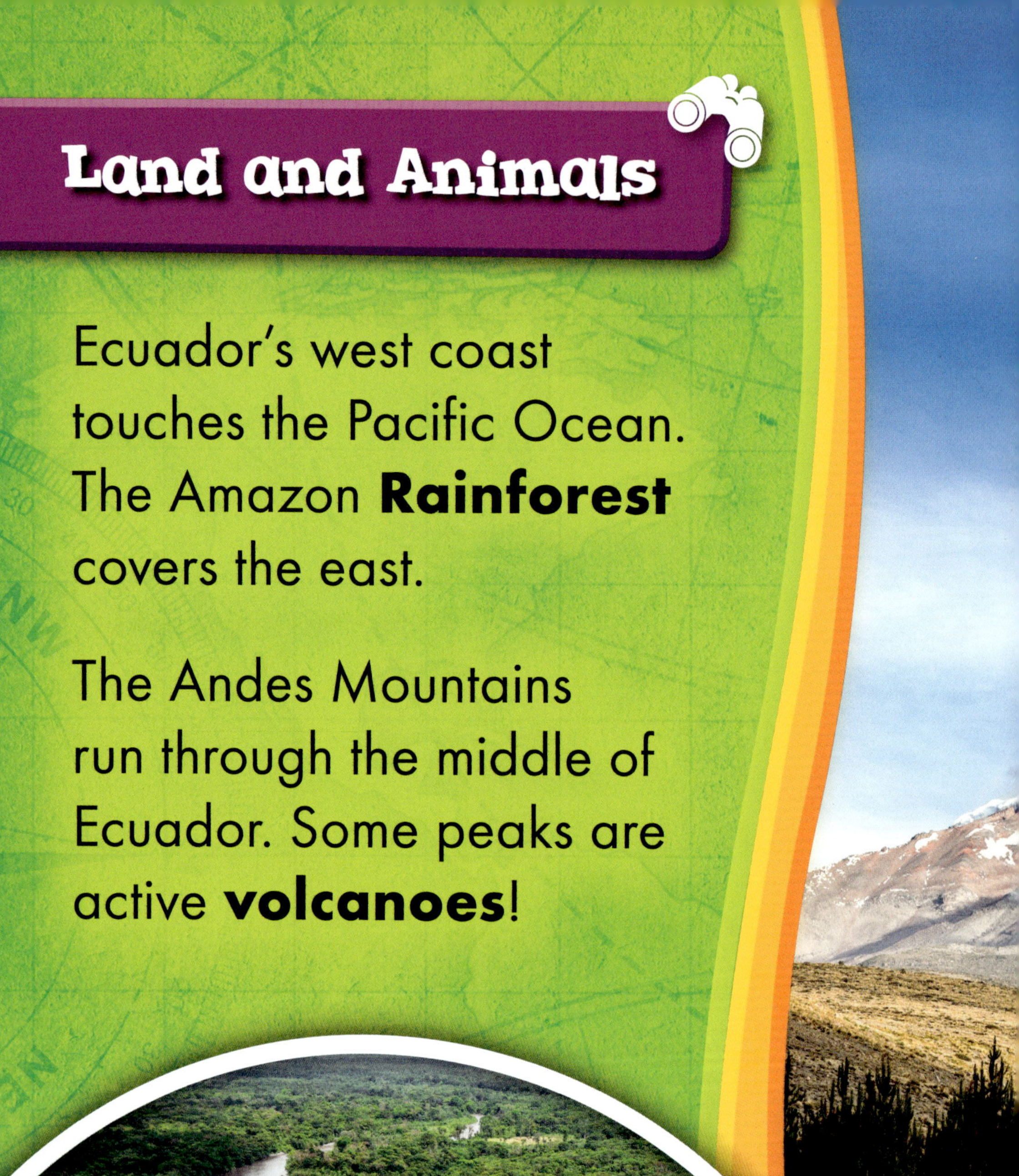

Amazon Rainforest

Mount Chimborazo

Size: 20,702 feet (6,310 meters) tall

Famous For: the tallest mountain in Ecuador and the point on Earth closest to outer space

Most of Ecuador is hot and **humid**. The mountains are cooler.

Ecuador has wet and dry seasons. Eastern Ecuador gets the most rain.

Condors fly over the Andes.
Groups of hillstars rest nearby.

Animals of Ecuador

Andean condor

Ecuadorian hillstar

jaguar

Galápagos penguin

Jaguars hunt in the rainforest. Penguins and giant tortoises walk the Galápagos Islands.

Life in Ecuador

Most Ecuadorians have both **Indigenous** and European backgrounds. Spanish is widely spoken.

Most people live in cities. **Extended family** often lives together in one home.

English: Hello
Spanish: Hola
(OH-lah)
TRADITIONAL

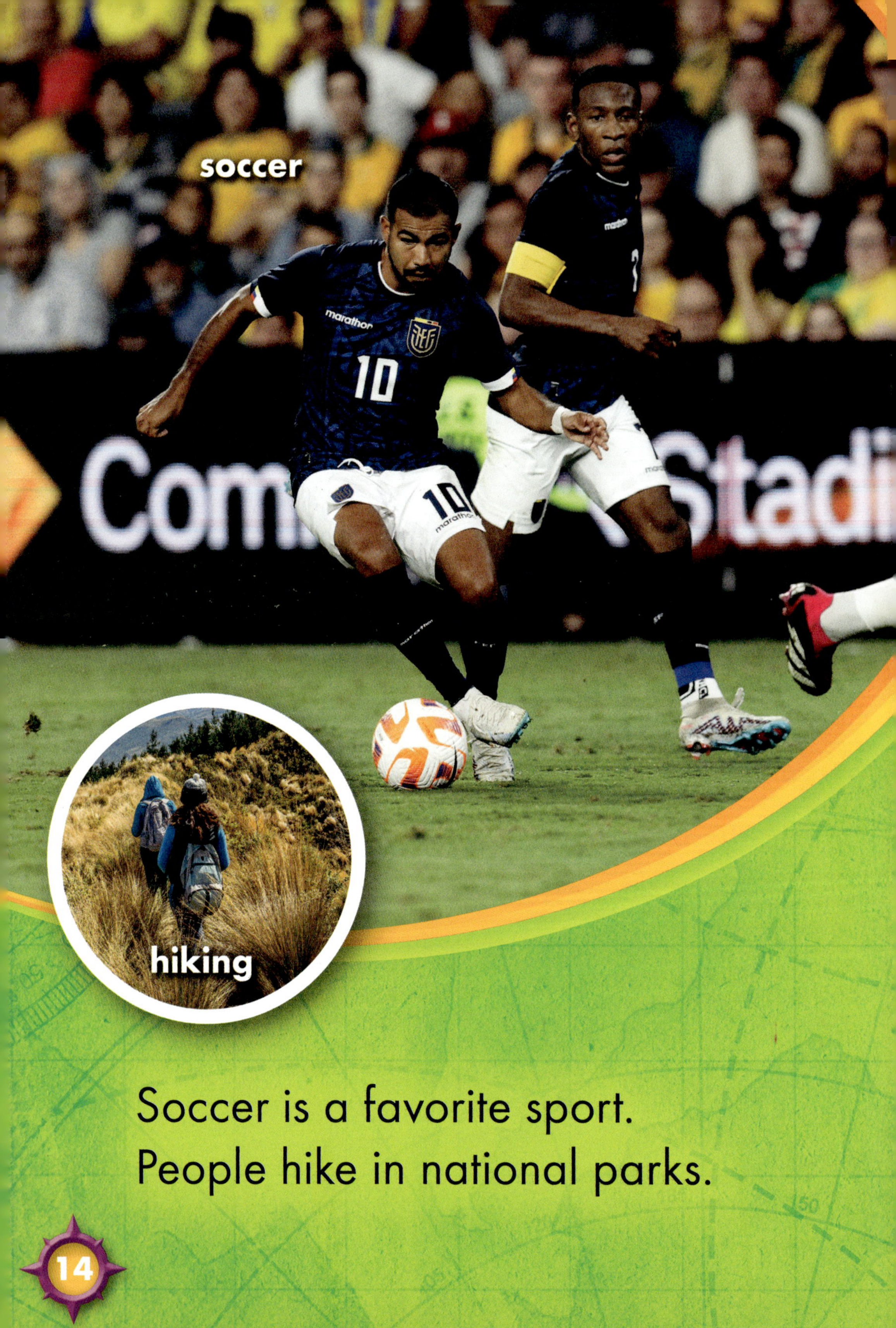

Soccer is a favorite sport.
People hike in national parks.

Many Ecuadorians enjoy live music! **Traditional** dances are a special part of **celebrations**.

Bolon de verde is a filling breakfast! Empanadas are a favorite snack.

Ecuadorian Foods

bolon de verde

empanadas

ceviche

espumilla

Ceviche is a common seafood dish. *Espumilla* is a dessert flavored with fresh fruit.

Carnaval takes place in February or March. Cities host parades with dancing and water fights!

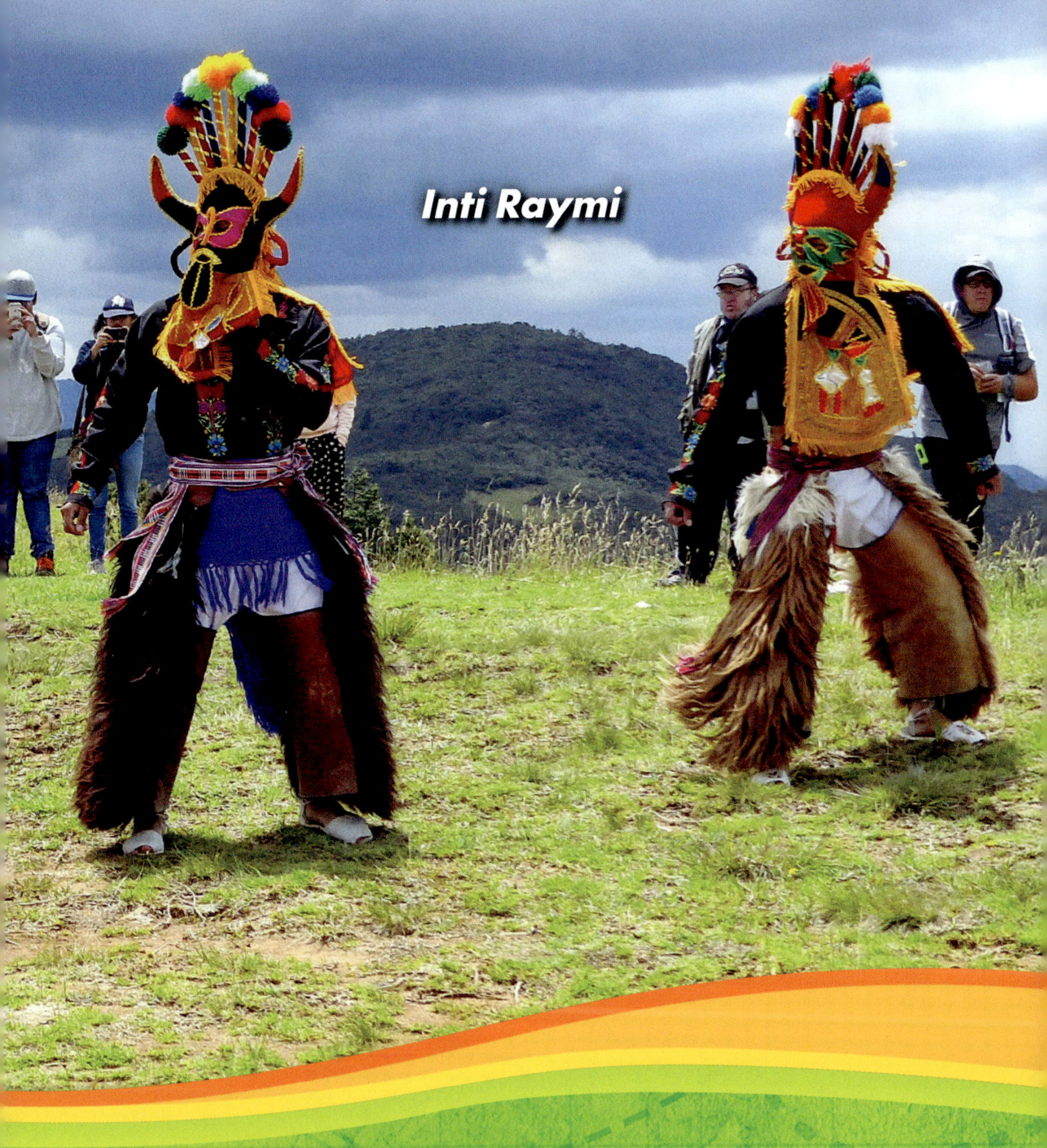

Inti Raymi is in June. Indigenous groups honor their **cultures**.

Ecuador Facts

Size:
109,484 square miles
(283,561 square kilometers)

Population:
18,309,984 (2024)

National Holiday:
Independence Day (August 10)

Main Language:
Spanish

Capital City:
Quito

Famous Face

Name: Ronnie Nader

Famous For: first-ever astronaut from Ecuador

other: 3%

Roman Catholic: 68%

other Christian: 21%

none: 8%

Top Landmarks

Galápagos Islands

Mitad del Mundo

Otavalo Market

Glossary

celebrations—special or fun activities for an event, occasion, or holiday

cultures—customs and beliefs of certain groups of people

equator—the imaginary line around the center of Earth

extended family—a family that includes parents, children, and other relatives such as grandparents, aunts, or uncles

humid—having a lot of water in the air

Indigenous—related to people originally from an area

rainforest—a thick, green forest that receives a lot of rain

traditional—related to customs, ideas, or beliefs handed down from one generation to the next

volcanoes—holes in the earth; when a volcano erupts, hot ash, gas, and melted rock called lava shoot out.

To Learn More

AT THE LIBRARY

Cords, Sarah Statz. *Your Passport to Ecuador.* North Mankato, Minn.: Capstone Press, 2021.

Jackson, Tom. *Galápagos.* New York, N.Y.: DK Publishing, 2022.

Pettiford, Rebecca. *Honduras.* Bloomington, Minn.: Bellwether Media, 2026.

ON THE WEB

FACTSURFER

Factsurfer.com gives you a safe, fun way to find more information.

1. Go to www.factsurfer.com.
2. Enter "Ecuador" into the search box and click 🔍.
3. Select your book cover to see a list of related content.

Index

The images in this book are reproduced through the courtesy of: Fotos593, front cover, p. 21 (Mitad del Mundo); railway fx, p. 3; Jess Kraft, pp. 4, 21 (Galápagos Islands); Curioso.Photography, p. 6; Jon Chica, pp. 6-7; Al Carrera, p. 8; Maris Maskalans, p. 9; Benjamint, p. 10; Don Mammoser, p. 11 (Andean condor); FotoRequest, p. 11 (Ecuadorian hillstar); Mark Green, p. 11 (jaguar); Todamo, p. 11 (Galápagos penguin); Michael Sparrow/ Alamy Stock Photo, p. 12; ireneuke, pp. 12-13, 17; IOIO IMAGES, p. 14 (top); SL-Photography, p. 14 (bottom); Octavio Parra, p. 15; CokyCP, p. 16 (bolon de verde); hlphoto, p. 16 (empanadas); Jose David Gutierrez, p. 16 (ceviche); Fabricio Burbano, p. 16 (espumilla); IRYNA KURILOVYCH, pp. 18-19; Ecuadorian Civilian Space Agency, p. 20; Omri Eliyahu, p. 21 (Otavalo Market); apple2499, p. 22.